The Longest Lent

Saying 'Yes' after a year of 'No'

D1416236

The Longest Lent

SAYING YES AFTER A YEAR OF NO

DAILY DEVOTIONS FOR LENT

DANIEL HAWKINS | MELISSA TURKETT | KATIE NEWKIRK

MEG WITMER-FAILE | SCOTT GOODFELLOW

TABLE OF CONTENTS

INTRODUCTION

As I stood under the covered drop-off at the back of Santa Fe Elementary School, I was surrounded and yet alone.

The gym that was six steps away was filled with faithful volunteers, pallets of food, caring educators, and excited school children. In just a few minutes family after family would come by as we shared food for the Spring Break holiday. People and their joy-filled noise were everywhere, and yet I was alone - isolated in my own world - as I tried (and frequently failed) to connect with my church's lay leadership on a six or seven-way FaceTime call with no wifi and a marginal cell connection.

It was Friday, March 13, and we were wrestling with the decision to host in-person worship or not for the first time.

THIS is when the COVID-19 pandemic hit home for me for the first time. In many ways this culminated a week where COVID-19 made its first impacts on many of us. The news began covering little else. Our TVs were filled with images coming out of New York and Italy. Many of the things that represent markers of "normal life" in the spring got upended. College conferences suspended their conference basketball tournaments. The NCAA canceled March Madness. The NBA and NHL suspended their seasons. Schools far and wide announced extended Spring Breaks. Employers began sending their employees home to work remotely. We made our first connection with Zoom.

Little did we know in those early March days just how much our lives would change in the months that followed. As the world was gripped tighter and tighter by a global pandemic, its ensuing lockdown and later stilted reopening, faced with imperfect choices the refrain of our leaders and our own conscience remained consistent... 'No.'

'No' to returning to traditional school after Spring Break

'No' to big weddings happening as planned

'No' to proms or graduations

'No' to seeing family, free of worry or guilt

'No' to handshakes, hugs and seeing smiles on faces

'No' to visiting sick friends in the hospital

'No' to a carefree life where we didn't have to worry about the air we were breathing

'No'

Again and again… 'No'

Throughout the history of Christianity, Lent has been a season of 'No.' It has been a season in which we, as followers of Jesus, have said 'No' to ourselves, our desires and our wants through fasting. Over the 40 days of

Lent, Christians offer personal sacrifices to prepare them for the new beginning Christ will bring at Easter.

As we approach Lent 2021, we do so after what could easily be categorized as the "world's longest Lent," a year of 'No.' While I am thankful for what has been our consistent and often faith-filled 'No,' I believe that this Lent is a time for us to offer a consistent and faith-filled 'Yes.'

In the pages that follow, you will be invited to explore, reflect and embody a series of faith-filled 'Yeses.'

Saying 'Yes' to Sabbath... after a year of lockdown

Saying 'Yes' to Healing… and wholeness: body, mind and spirit

Saying 'Yes' to Praying... for our enemies

Saying 'Yes' to Reading the Bible... between the lines

Saying 'Yes' to Restoring... relationships with others

Saying 'Yes' to entering the story

These 'Yeses' aren't intended to take us back to where we were on March 12, 2020. That option doesn't exist for us. When we say 'Yes' in the days to come, we are saying 'Yes' to Christ and preparing ourselves for the *new beginning* Christ is bringing out of this year of 'No.'

I am deeply thankful for the faithful friends and colleagues who have helped shape this Lenten devotional. I believe that I can speak for us all when I say that we thank you for being on this journey with us, and we invite you to invest deeply. We believe and trust that when you do, you will find the *new beginning* Christ is bringing out of this year of 'No.'

Rev. Daniel Hawkins, Editor

The Longest Lent

ASH WEDNESDAY

Yet even now, says the Lord, return to me with all your hearts, with fasting, with weeping, and with sorrow; tear your hearts and not your clothing.
Return to the Lord your God, for he is merciful and compassionate, very patient, full of faithful love, and ready to forgive.
Joel 2:12-13

"Hey Preacher… What happened to your truck?"

What had happened to my truck???

While I don't want to fulfill too many stereotypes about young Texas men, it is safe to say that I loved that truck. I had wanted one ever since I turned 16, and as a young pastor in my mid-twenties, I was very proud of my Texas Edition F-150. It was big, tough, and could haul heavy stuff (all of the identifying characteristics that my 16-year-old self had liked to claim).

This truck had been with me during my earlier days of fatherhood. It had hauled my family and all of our stuff to the mountains for vacations, and had hauled lumber and concrete when we built a deck off the back end of our house. When I was leading a church plant, it had pulled a trailer every week filled to the brim with pipe and drape, speakers, cables, light bars, hospitality stations, and even a changing table for the nursery.

For the decade I had this truck, it was a part of my life nearly every day. So, when someone walked into the church one day and poked their head in my office and asked that question, it caught my attention.

I followed them back out to the parking lot. When they pointed at the Ford logo on my tailgate, I was relieved. "Oh that." I said. "It's been getting that way for a while."

What they wanted to share with me about my truck was that it had lost its identity. All of the contrasting blue and black in the logo had been worn away by thousands of miles on the road, and all that was left was a nondescript chrome oval. I knew it was a Ford, but you could no longer see that it was a Ford just by looking at the tailgate.

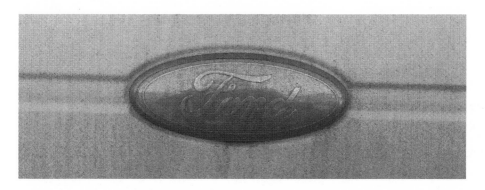

In the days that followed that trip to the parking lot, I began to reflect on that nondescript oval. While we don't have logos emblazoned upon us in the same way that my truck did, we do have an identity, and this identity should be as visibly evident to the world around us as the Ford logo was on my tailgate the day the truck rolled off of the assembly line.

On this day when we go to our churches (or church parking lots) and have a cross of ash emblazoned on our foreheads, we return to God and encounter our identity in its fullness. We see the truth that, at times, our logo too has been worn down by the miles and struggles of a year of 'No.'

In the coarsely ground ashes we see that we are mortal. We confess our sin. We repent of our failing.

On this day when we go to our churches and have a cross of ash emblazoned on our foreheads, we return to God and encounter our identity in its fullness. We see the truth that, no matter how long the year, no matter how faded the logo, no matter how deep the struggle, we belong to Christ.

In the shape of the cross we see that we are forgiven, loved and freed by his love.

As we enter into this Lenten journey and explore how we can say 'Yes' after a year of 'No,' may we enter with burnt ash on our heads, hope in our hearts, and a commitment to make our identity more and more visible by the day.

THURSDAY

"John the Baptist was in the wilderness calling for people to be baptized to show that they were changing their hearts and lives and wanted God to forgive their sins."
Mark 1:4

REFLECTION:

"[…] we must submit to change if we would be formed into this cruciform faith. We may come singing "Just as I Am," but we will not stay by being our same old selves."[1]   *- Will Willimon*

#SAYYESTODAY:

As the ash fades from our foreheads today, remember the call of Christ is to a baptism that changes hearts and lives. Spend time with this question: "How am I different today because I said 'Yes' to following

---

[1] William Willimon, Bread and Wine: Readings for Lent and Easter, 9.

Jesus?" Jot down notes. Talk with someone close to you. Reflect and share.

PRAYER:

Loving God, you are the gift that is beyond measure, and you offer to us all the gift of new beginnings. Over the days that come, during this Lent, help me to say 'Yes' over and over again to the new life you are inviting me into.

Amen.

FRIDAY

"I offer my life to you, Lord. My God, I trust you."
Psalm 25:1-2a

REFLECTION:

"I want to walk as a child of the light
I want to follow Jesus
God sent the stars to give light to the world
The star of my life is Jesus
In Him, there is no darkness at all
The night and the day are both alike
The Lamb is the light of the city of God
Shine in my heart, Lord Jesus"[2] *- Kathleen Thomerson*

---

[2] Kathleen Thomerson, United Methodist Hymnal #206

20

#SAYYESTODAY:

As the dusk of evening falls today, grab a flashlight, and go for a walk. As you walk, allow the light of your flashlight to lead the way. As you walk, notice the light that surrounds you - the stars and the moon... the streetlamp and headlights. Allow it to be a reminder of the presence of Christ in your everyday life. Thank God for the light in your life.

PRAYER:

Shine in my heart, Lord Jesus!

In this season of prolonged struggle, pain, frustration and 'No,' shine your light, O God. Shine it bright so that I might be aware of your presence with me this day.

Amen.

SATURDAY

"Be careful that you don't practice your religion in front of people to draw their attention. If you do, you will have no reward from your Father who is in heaven. Whenever you give to the poor, don't blow your trumpet as the hypocrites do in the synagogues and in the streets so that they may get praise from people. I assure you, that's the only reward they'll get."

Matthew 6:1-2

REFLECTION:

"It is well know that Christ consistently used the expression 'follower.' He never asks for admirers, worshipers, or adherents. No, he calls disciples. It is not adherents of a teaching but followers of a life Christ is looking for."[3]
- Soren Kierkegaard

#SAYYESTODAY:

Read Matthew 6:1-18.

---

[3] Soren Kierkegaard, Bread and Wine: Readings for Lent and Easter, 55.

Tomorrow we will begin our first week of saying 'Yes' after a year of 'No,' and over the coming days we will put our faith into action in many much needed ways. Today God invites us to ground ourselves in our "why." Reflect on why am I ready to say 'Yes'? Whose glory do I seek? Who do I intend to follow?

PRAYER:

"Pray like this: Our Father who is in heaven, uphold the holiness of your name. Bring in your kingdom so that your will is done on earth as it's done in heaven. Give us the bread we need for today. Forgive us for the ways we have wronged you, just as we also forgive those who have wronged us. And don't lead us into temptation, but rescue us from the evil one."[4]

Amen.

---

[4] Matthew 6:9-13 CEB

The Longest Lent

Saying 'Yes' to Sabbath... after a year of lockdown

First Sunday of Lent

After a year of staying home, haven't we had more than our fair share of rest? Haven't we taken a break from "all the things" long enough? After a year of lockdown, do we really need to say 'Yes' to Sabbath? These are questions you may be wondering and understandably so. With Sabbath literally meaning "to rest" or "to cease," this could be seen as a year of Sabbath in many ways. And many of us are over it.

In March 2020, in quite a hectic whirlwind, our lives drastically changed before our eyes. NBA games were cancelled, cruise ships were stranded, schools moved to virtual classrooms, and we began to worship through a screen. We entered into lockdown, many of us mandated to stay home to save lives. Since that time, as the cancellation of sporting events, weddings, graduations, and trips began to grow, we have been living in a season of forced rest.

For many of us, this past year has been a much slower pace of life than ever before. For those who are retired, many of the activities, social gatherings, and church events you had planned have either been cancelled altogether or relegated to Zoom. For those who have been furloughed or let go because of the COVID crisis, your days that used to fly by with the hustle and bustle of work are now dragging on at a sloth's pace. Most all of our weekends look a lot different than they used to, with significantly fewer plans on the schedule. Instead of going to concerts, sporting events, birthday parties, and church potlucks, our weekends are now filled with binge watching TV, puzzles, and social distanced driveway chats with the neighbors.

I must acknowledge that this forced rest is not across the board. For some of us, this past year has been the most frantic year of our lives. For those who work in healthcare, you have been pushing mental and physical limits, working overtime to care for overcrowded hospitals. For teachers, this year has been exhausting trying to be an educator, mentor, technology specialist, counselor, emotion scientist, nurse, and mediator all at once. For those working from home while trying to parent and homeschool children, "rest" is a foreign concept, a long-lost dream. For leaders of businesses and organizations, this year has been chaotic trying to adapt to all the change and make tough decisions.

Whether this year has felt like an overflow of rest or whether your cup is running dry because of almost no rest, I invite you to #sayyestoday to Sabbath. And here's why. We are all worn down and weary mentally, physically, emotionally, and spiritually from this trying and traumatic past year. And Sabbath rest is what fills our cups up and renews our weary souls. We all need Sabbath. We all need to be revived.

There is a difference between the forced rest brought on by the pandemic and Sabbath rest. The forced rest of the pandemic has pushed us to fill our days with activities that often do the opposite of renewing us, they drain us. We scroll through social media for hours only to realize that we feel worse afterwards than before. In our boredom, we spend too much time and money online shopping to buy things we don't need, only to regret it when our credit card bill comes. We stuff our faces with Buddy the Elf levels of sweets intake, knowing it will make us sick. We spend our days glued to the news, though it only makes us more agitated and anxious.

Sabbath rest does not drain our cup, rather it refills our cup. Sabbath is a particular kind of rest; it is a rest in God, a rest that renews, a rest that cultivates joy. As Rob Bell notes, Sabbath is a day to remember that "we are human beings not human doings."[5]

---

[5] Rob Bell, Twitter, September 26, 2009, https://twitter.com/realrobbell/status/4393436736?lang=en.

There is a reason that Genesis 2 talks about how God created the earth in six days and on the seventh day rested. There is a reason that after God rescued the Israelites as slaves in Egypt, where they labored from sunrise to sunset seven days a week, that God incorporated a command to keep the Sabbath for one day a week. Sabbath is not a means to an end; a brief break so we can get back to work. Sabbath is the end, the culmination of creation. Abraham Heschel asserts, "The Sabbath is not for the sake of the weekdays; the weekdays are for the sake of the Sabbath. It is not an interlude but the climax of living."[6] The ceasing of labor creates space for us to have the fullness of life in God.

When you imagine a day of rest that actually fills your cup and connects you to God, what comes to mind for you? Perhaps it is a long walk or bike ride, letting the sun warm your skin and the crisp air fill your lungs. Perhaps it is curling up in your favorite chair with a freshly

6 Abraham Heschel, The Sabbath, 3.

sharpened pencil in hand, drawing or journaling prayers. Perhaps it is enjoying a favorite meal, with your family at the dinner table, the conversation intermingled with laughter and deep ponderings. Perhaps it is taking a nap on the couch, with your dog curled up beside you. Perhaps it is practicing yoga, finding God in the humble child's pose.

God delights in our rest and our play. God delights in our joy. May you say 'Yes' to Sabbath this week, and may that 'Yes' bring you fullness of life. For God gave us Sabbath as not only a command, but also a gift—a gift to restore us and rest in God.

MONDAY

"The Lord is my shepherd, I shall not want. He makes me lie down in green pastures; he leads me beside still waters; he restores my soul."
Psalm 23:1-2, NRSV

REFLECTION:

"A world without a Sabbath would be like a man without a smile, like summer without flowers, and like a homestead without a garden. It is the most joyous day of the week."[7]   *- Henry Ward Beecher*

#SAYYESTODAY:

Spend an hour today outside in nature. In that hour, take a break from technology, and recognize God's presence in creation. Take notice of the trees, the sky, the scents, and the air you breathe. Allow God to restore your soul, as you spend time outdoors.

---

[7] Henry Ward Beecher, Royal Truths.

PRAYER:

Dear God, thank you for being my shepherd, who shows me green pastures to rest by and leads me beside still waters. Thank you for the gift of your creation to remind me of your presence and love. As I rest in you this day, restore my soul. Fill my cup until it overflows with your peace and joy.

Amen.

TUESDAY

"I thank you because you answered me, because you were my saving help. The stone rejected by the builders is now the main foundation stone! This has happened because of the Lord; it is astounding in our sight! This is the day the Lord acted; we will rejoice and celebrate in it!"
Psalm 118:21-24

REFLECTION:

"You need those days... when you are reminded that efficacy and production are not the divine's highest goals for your life... If you do not have the celebration, if you do not have the ceasing from labor, then you do not have the fullness of life."[8]
- Rob Bell

---

[8] Rob Bell, "Menuha!," Robcast, podcast audio, August 13, 2018, https://podcasts.apple.com/us/podcast/the-robcast/id956742638.

#SAYYESTODAY:

Write down five things in your life that bring you joy. Do one of those things today.

PRAYER:

God of Joy, this is the day you have made, and I will rejoice and be glad in it! For laughter at the dinner table, for watching the sunset on a walk, and for music that makes me smile, I give you thanks. Restore to me a joy that is found in you alone this day.

Amen.

WEDNESDAY

"Be still, and know that I am God! I am exalted among the nations, I am exalted in the earth."
Psalm 46:10

REFLECTION:

"Solitude is the place of purification and transformation, the place of the great struggle and the great encounter."[9]   *- Henri Nouwen*

#SAYYESTODAY:

Sabbath is a time to rest in God. Solitude is one spiritual practice that helps us rest in God. Today, I invite you to spend five minutes in silence, listening to God. Take today's 'Yes' a step further by downloading the *Centering Prayer* app on your phone, which takes you through a guided

---

[9] Henri J. M. Nouwen, The Spiritual Life: Eight Essential Titles by Henri Nouwen, 20.

centering prayer. Centering prayer is a type of prayer that is focused completely on the presence of God.

Prayer:

Speak, Lord, for your servant is listening. Open my ears to hear your still small voice in the silence. Open my heart to receive the nudges of your Spirit. Speak, Lord, for your servant is listening.

Amen.

THURSDAY

"Then [Jesus] said to them, "Is it legal on the Sabbath to do good or to do evil, to save life or to kill?" But they said nothing. Looking around at them with anger, deeply grieved at their unyielding hearts, he said to the man, "Stretch out your hand." So he did, and his hand was made healthy."
Mark 3:4-5

REFLECTION:

"Let no one ever come to you without leaving better and happier. Be the living expression of God's kindness: kindness in your face, kindness in your eyes, kindness in your smile."[10]   - Mother Teresa

#SAYYESTODAY:

One meaningful practice to consider incorporating into your Sabbath is an act of kindness. Acts of kindness bring joy both to others and yourself.

---

[10] John Templeton, Worldwide Laws of Life: 200 Eternal Spiritual Principles, 448.

Be the good you wish to see in the world by engaging in one intentional act of kindness today. Here are some potential ideas to try: drop cookies off at a neighbor's house, pay for a stranger's order, give an extra restaurant tip with an encouragement note, pick up litter on the street, or send a card to someone who needs encouragement.

PRAYER:

Dear God, you are good, and you work all things together for good. Empower me today to come alongside you in the work you are doing in our world. Show me the ways in which you are calling me to do good and to act kindly in your name.

Amen.

FRIDAY

"The Lord said, 'Go out and stand at the mountain before the Lord. The Lord is passing by.' A very strong wind tore through the mountains and broke apart the stones before the Lord. But the Lord wasn't in the wind. After the wind, there was an earthquake. But the Lord wasn't in the earthquake. After the earthquake, there was a fire. But the Lord wasn't in the fire. After the fire, there was a sound. Thin. Quiet."
1 Kings 19:11-12

REFLECTION:

"Sabbath is that uncluttered time and space in which we can distance ourselves from our own activities enough to see what God is doing."[11]
- Eugene Peterson

---

[11] Eugene Peterson, The Pastor's Guide to Personal Spiritual Formation, 134.

#SAYYESTODAY:

Spend a few minutes reflecting, and perhaps even journaling, your thoughts on the question, "Where did I see God today?" Did you see God in the smile and giggles of a child? Or the welcome of your dog, as you entered the door? Did you see God in the face of the cashier at the store? Or perhaps in the face of one asking you for help? Where did you see God's face today?

PRAYER:

O Holy Spirit, in the noise and chaos of my day, it's hard to hear you, let alone see you working. Yet, I know you are there. You are here. Always here. Quiet the noise, the to-do list, and the anxious thoughts whirling through my mind. In the stillness, make me more aware of your presence. In Jesus' name, **Amen**.

SATURDAY

"Remember the Sabbath day and treat it as holy. Six days you may work and do all your tasks, but the seventh day is a Sabbath to the Lord your God. Do not do any work on it—not you, your sons or daughters, your male or female servants, your animals, or the immigrant who is living with you."

Exodus 20:8-10

REFLECTION:

"Test the premise that you are worth more than what you can produce- that even if you spend one whole day being good for nothing you would still be precious in God's sight- and when you get anxious because you are convinced that this is not so, remember that your own conviction is not required. This is a commandment. Your worth has already been established, even when you are not working."[12]
- Barbara Brown Taylor

---

[12] Barbara Brown Taylor, An Altar in the World, 139.

#SAYYESTODAY:

Practice Sabbath today. Do not do any work today. Instead, spend the day resting and engaging in activities that help you to rest in God, restore your soul, and bring you joy.

PRAYER:

Gracious God, thank you for the gift of Sabbath. Thank you for the gift of a day to rest and be renewed in you. Not only that, but thank you for setting an example of rest. Today, I rest because you rested. May you be honored in my rest and play this day.

Amen.

Saying 'Yes' to Healing... and Wholeness: Body, Mind & Spirit

Second Sunday of Lent

Several years ago, my husband, Tom, and I attended a Five Day Academy for Spiritual Formation retreat at the Roslyn Retreat Center in Richmond, Virginia. It was an intentional time of rest and renewal within a disciplined Christian community that followed a daily rhythm of morning, midday and evening prayer, Holy Communion, silence, worship, study, rest, and reflection. For me, it was also a time of healing and introspection. At the time, I was struggling on several levels: a broken relationship with someone I had trusted and respected, and the terminal illness of a dear friend. Intuitively, I recognized the need to nurture my spirit, to be vulnerable to the emotional brokenness I was experiencing, and to embrace steps that would lead me to my own healing and wholeness. I know that I have the capacity to heal. For me, that means befriending my pain and brokenness, resting with it, and becoming reconciled to it, while leaning into hope and love.

Our faculty presenters for the retreat were two writers whose work I had read, wrestled with, and admired—Robert Benson and Roberta Bondi. I was delighted to be in their presence and to have this much-needed sacred time to nurture my soul and embrace healing. So, it seemed timely when Robert Benson referred to this passage from his book *Living Prayer*, in one of his lectures:

"To embrace one's brokenness, whatever it looks like, whatever has caused it, carries within it the possibility that one might come to embrace one's healing, and then one might come to the next step: to embrace another and their brokenness and their possibility for being healed. To avoid one's brokenness is to turn one's

back on the possibility that the Healer might be at work here, perhaps for you, perhaps for another."[13]

These words came back to me as I have been reflecting on the "Saying 'Yes' to Healing" Lenten focus. It reminded me how necessary it is to embrace my brokenness, and to ask God for the strength, courage, vulnerability, and patience that this journey to wholeness requires. Turning my back on my need for healing seems presumptuous and ungrateful. Yes, I need healing: from fractured and broken relationships, from the loss of loved ones, from harmful words and actions I have received and also spoken. In truth, I seek a wholeness that allows me to become the best version of myself—a beloved child of God. I also recognize that this path toward healing is not a solitary journey. I am accompanied by the Holy Spirit, by the love of family and friends, by Scripture and sacred texts, by the works of gifted authors, poets, artists, and musicians, by deep conversations and laughter, and by the

---

[13] Robert Benson, Living Prayer, 46.

astounding beauty of God's creation. Hope resides in the healing power of the Divine—may my heart be open to this healing and wholeness.

"Healing" can have many meanings, of course. Perhaps our first thought when we hear this word is being cured of a disease or illness. In this season of COVID-19, we pray for healing, for a cure to this deadly virus that has already infected millions of people, and from which hundreds of thousands in our country, alone, have died. For anyone who is suffering from any health concern, the prayer is often for healing and for a cure. The Bible is filled with stories of miraculous healing, especially in the Gospels, where we encounter Jesus as a great healer, healing the sick, the diseased, the blind, the deaf, and the paralyzed. We also read of him healing the brokenhearted and the lost, liberating the oppressed, and preaching good news to the poor. We know that God heals, though the mystery of how and when healing occurs is unknown to us. Through modern science we may be cured of physical sickness, but the sickness of the soul, that healing is of God. It is this healing, this wholeness we long

46

for. "Heal me, O LORD, and I shall be healed. Save me, and I shall be saved." Jeremiah 17:14a NRSV

Elizabeth Kübler-Ross notes that, "Healing does not necessarily mean to become physically well or to be able to get up and walk around again. Rather, it means achieving a balance between the physical, emotional, intellectual, and spiritual dimensions....".   So, in addition to 'curing', healing has a deeper, more holistic meaning. In prayer and sacred silence, we may discover that the healing we need is not a physical cure, but a healing of the heart. Perhaps the healing we seek is rooted in the woundedness of a broken relationship, the death of a loved one, or the loss of identity, place, purpose, or meaning in our life.   Healing is the process of refusing to remain wounded—a process that takes courage, love, and hope.

"Healing depends on wanting to be well. I may not forget the blows I have suffered in life, but I must choose not to live under their power forever. Most of all, I must not choose to imprison myself in my own pain. Whatever has

47

*mutilated us — the betrayal, the dishonesty, the mockery, the broken promises —
there is more to life than that."*[14]   *Sister Joan Chittister*

In the past year, we have experienced loss on so many levels: being in community, worship, shopping, spending time with family and friends, going out to eat, or traveling. We have also been touched by isolation, sickness and death from the COVID-19 virus. Life today is very different than it was this time last year, before the pandemic spread into our lives and households. In response to this new normal, we have leaned into our creativity to find new ways to be in community and to stay connected with family, friends, and colleagues. We have spent more time physically separated from people, and so perhaps the healing we seek is from being isolated and alone; a return to being in community, a return to some sense of 'normalcy.'

---

[14] Sister Joan Chittister, from For Everything there is a Season (Orbis)

There is also healing needed for people who have caused or suffered indignities of discrimination; for those who have been ostracized, marginalized, or oppressed; yes, healing is needed.

During this Lenten season, you are invited to explore places of healing, some of which you may be aware of and some you have chosen to forget. Perhaps some of your healing is wrapped up in complicated grief. Where are the places you desire healing? What prayers and needs are you placing before God? How are you giving God thanks and praise for the healing that has taken place in your life and in the lives of others? How are you participating in and contributing to the healing around you and within you? What resources will you turn to for inspiration and encouragement in this time: a long walk, conversation with friends, writing, art, music, dance, reading poetry, sacred texts or something new? In what places are you willing to open up, experience vulnerability, and listen for the guidance of the Holy Spirit?

It is my prayer that this week's Scriptures, indeed this entire Lenten journey, will challenge, encourage, and comfort you as you prayerfully consider saying 'Yes' to healing and wholeness in your life. It is a journey, and you are never alone—may we walk together.

God is with us—thanks be to God!

MWF

MONDAY

"Praise the LORD! Because it is good to sing praise to our God! Because it is a pleasure to make beautiful praise! The Lord rebuilds Jerusalem, gathering up Israel's exiles. God heals the brokenhearted and bandages their wounds."
Psalm 147:1-3

REFLECTION:

"There is healing in the universe. There is fabric that holds things together. When it is ready…in it's own good time, shall it not bind together…all of us?"[15]
       - Clair McDermott

"For every thing there is a season, and a time for every matter under heaven… a time to heal…" Ecclesiastes 3:1, 3b NRSV

---

[15] Clair McDermott, The Wave, Friends of Silence, June 2011, vol. XXIV, No.6.

#SAYYESTODAY:

Read Psalm 147 and consider the ways God has been present in your life, and in the lives of others, offering healing, comfort, reassurance, and protection. Also consider that after spending forty days in the wilderness and being tempted by the devil, Jesus returned to Nazareth and entered the synagogue on the Sabbath. He was handed the scroll of Isaiah that read, "The Spirit of the Lord is upon me, because the Lord has anointed me to preach the gospel to the poor. He has sent me to heal the brokenhearted, to preach deliverance to the captives, and recovering sight to the blind, to set at liberty those who are oppressed."(Luke 4:18, NIV)

What is your prayerful response to Psalm 147 and to Luke 4:18?

How might these readings frame your week of 'Saying 'Yes' to Healing'?

PRAYER:

Creator God, you are the only source of health and healing. In you there is calm and the only true peace in the universe. You heal the brokenhearted, you hold us in our suffering. In you, there is assurance and calm. Grant to each one of us an awareness of your Holy Spirit and the assurance of your presence in all times and places. When we are tired, anxious, angry, hurt, wounded, and impatient, teach us to yield ourselves to your unfailing love and compassion. May we be surrounded by your power and your presence, and may we place our trust in you.

Amen.

TUESDAY

"As he entered a village, ten men with skin diseases approached him. Keeping their distance from him, they raised their voices and said, "Jesus, Master, show us mercy!" When Jesus saw them, he said, "Go, show yourselves to the priests." As they left, they were cleansed. One of them, when he saw that he had been healed, returned, and praised God in a loud voice."

Luke 17: 12-15

REFLECTION:

Surely each of us has cried out for mercy, for healing, for help...cries born of pain, woundedness, suffering, grief, isolation, cries of fear or weariness. We recall Jesus crying out from the cross, "Eloi, Eloi, lema sabachthani"...My God, my God, why have you forsaken me?" (Matthew 27:46 NRSV) We are comforted knowing that God hears our cries and is present with us.

How often have we felt God's presence through friends, family, and even strangers—angels in our midst?

#SAYYESTODAY:

Read Luke 17:12-19, and prayerfully consider how God empowers us to hear the cries of the suffering, to step across boundaries and extend mercy to outsiders. May we be people who pay attention to the suffering around us and choose to be part of the healing of our world, and may we be grateful people who fall on our knees giving God thanks and praise for our healing.

Prayer:

Loving God, even in difficult times we choose our response to the suffering we encounter. May we respond as the grateful Samaritan, with open eyes, receptive hearts, recognizing God's powerful love in Christ Jesus. May we return, fall on our knees, and give God praise and thanksgiving! May we be witnesses of God's healing by sharing the Gospel—for it is in this expression of love that we are truly saved and made whole.

Amen.

WEDNESDAY

"A Samaritan, who was on a journey, came to where the man was. But when he saw him, he was moved with compassion. The Samaritan went to him and bandaged his wounds, tending them with oil and wine. Then he placed the wounded man on his own donkey, took him to an inn, and took care of him."
Luke 10:33-34

REFLECTION:

"The parable of the Good Samaritan is not about the curing of one person, it is about the healing of two, both of whom carry the scars of abuse, both of whom reside in us in tandem at all times. The Samaritan, by reaching out and touching the pain of another, opens life to new significance."[16]
- Sister Joan Chittister

---

[16] Sister Joan Chittister, from For Everything there is a Season, (Orbis)

#SAYYESTODAY:

As you read this passage from Luke, consider the healing that occurs when we are present with those who are suffering and sick, praying with and for them. Perhaps God is calling you to the healing ministry by serving on a prayer team or participating in a service of healing. Any healing we experience—physical, emotional, relational, or spiritual— occurs by way of the love and grace of God. The Holy Spirit is powerfully present as we kneel and pray for those in need of healing. While we recognize that in healing a specific cure may not happen, we place our faith and trust in God to comfort us, bless us, and make us whole.

PRAYER:

God of love and mercy, I need your healing touch today and every day. Please hear my prayers, be present with me, and forgive my shortcomings and failures. Help me recognize and embrace my woundedness of body, mind, spirit, and relationships. Give me the strength, the courage, and the desire to embark on my journey toward wholeness. Divine Healer, your love is beyond my comprehension; in you I place my trust, faith, and hope.

Amen.

THURSDAY

"Some men were bringing a man who was paralyzed, lying on a cot. They wanted to carry him in and place him before Jesus, but they couldn't reach him because of the crowd. So they took him up on the roof and lowered him — cot and all — through the roof tiles into the crowded room in front of Jesus. When Jesus saw their faith, he said, "Friend, your sins are forgiven."
Luke 5:18-20

REFLECTION:

"Where there is sorrow, there is holy ground"   *- Oscar Wilde*

I wonder if the paralyzed man had given up hope of being healed. I wonder if the size of the crowds around Jesus caused him despair, knowing he would never be able to get close to this healer, Jesus. But friends showed up to help and were not deterred by the crowds. They saw possibility where others did not. Their faithful persistence was hope in action that led to healing and forgiveness.

59

#SAYYESTODAY:

Today, read Luke 5:17-26, and consider how family, friends and community are present in our healing. Who has been present with you during a difficult time? Who have you walked with through their woundedness and pain? How have you experienced hope, forgiveness, and the presence of the Holy Spirit through community, family, friends, and even strangers?

PRAYER:

Holy One, we give thanks for the people who walk beside us on our journey, for their friendship, for their faithfulness, for their support. We give thanks for the ways they hold us accountable and help us recognize ways to overcome barriers to healing and new life. May we respond to their guidance with love, gratitude, and grace. May we, in turn, walk alongside others on their journey to healing and wholeness.

Amen.

FRIDAY

"When Jesus saw him lying there, knowing that he had already been there a long time, he asked him, "Do you want to get well?" The sick man answered him, "Sir, I don't have anyone who can put me in the water when it is stirred up. When I'm trying to get to it, someone else has gotten in ahead of me."
John 5:6-7

REFLECTION:

"Healing is embracing what is most feared;
Healing is opening what has been closed,
Softening what has hardened into obstruction.
Healing is learning to trust life."   *- Jean Achterberg*

#SAYYESTODAY:

Today read John 5: 1-9, 14-15. Is there an area in your life that has been less than whole and healthy?

Consider what barriers might be blocking your healing. Sometimes we make excuses, blame others, are angry, frustrated and convinced the world is out to get us. Perhaps, we are afraid and resist doing the hard work of looking within and facing our brokenness. Sometimes we just give up; we lose hope because we cannot imagine a future in which we are restored and whole. Today, invite the Holy Spirit to help you prayerfully discern your next steps toward wholeness—body, mind, spirit.

PRAYER:

Almighty and everlasting God, creator of our body, mind, and spirit, hear us as we pray. Enfold us in your love, your mercy, and your grace so that we may be healed, restored, and renewed to serve you, to love you, and to love our neighbor. **Amen.**

SATURDAY

"The Lord is my shepherd, I shall not want. He makes me lie down in green pastures; he leads me beside still waters; he restores my soul. He leads me in the paths of righteousness for his name's sake."
Psalm 23: 1-3, NRSV

REFLECTION:

God's good and faithful love is sufficient for every need. Trusting in God's presence, in God's care, in God's grace and mercy—all of this is a source of comfort and healing. Even in the most difficult times, in brokenness, in search for healing and wholeness, God is always there; we are never alone. Hope abides.

"Hope is the thing with feathers that perches in the soul and sings the tune without the words and never stops at all."[17]   *- Emily Dickinson*

---

[17] Barbara Brown Taylor, An Altar in the World, 139.

63

#SAYYESTODAY:

As we close out this week's Lenten focus on 'Saying 'Yes' to Healing', you are invited to spend time reading, meditating, praying, and contemplating Psalm 23. As you spend time with this Psalm, reading it several times, consider what word or phrase stands out to you. What might you hear God saying to you? How might God be calling you to respond to what God has placed on your heart? What are your next steps toward healing?

PRAYER:

Creator God, Source of all that is good and true, hear our prayer for healing of body, of mind, and of spirit. We are ever grateful for your love, your mercy, and your grace. Forgive us when we stray from you. May we be attentive to your voice; may we heed your calling on our lives; and may we be strengthened, encouraged, and sustained for the work you place before us. Healing is rooted in love. May we embrace our brokenness with courage and love, and may we be open to our individual woundedness, so that we may better understand the woundedness of those around us. May we partner with you in our healing, surrendering to you, forgiving ourselves and others, and imagining a new way of living and serving you, as we journey toward healing and wholeness. We offer this prayer in the name of Christ Jesus, **Amen**.

Healing... and Wholeness: body, mind and spirit

SAYING 'YES' TO PRAYING... FOR OUR ENEMIES

THIRD SUNDAY OF LENT

"How did we end up with THEM in our section???"

As I sat there on that early fall day, so much was familiar.

The firm steel bench below me, the press of humanity all around me, the warm sun on my face, the charged energy in the air, and the smell of Dr. Pepper and popcorn all told me that I was home... or at least I was at the home of the Baylor Bears, Floyd Casey Stadium. Just like many other Saturdays in the fall of my childhood, this Saturday I found myself sitting with my family at the forty yard line, ready to cheer on our Baylor Bears.

So much was familiar, but something was different. As I looked around the section we were sitting in, a section filled with members of my dad's law firm and their families, I saw lots of green and gold, but I also saw burnt orange and white.

How did that happen? I didn't understand. Their presence didn't compute in my young mind.

While I didn't know a whole lot about the economics of college sports, I had heard my parents talk enough to know that our tickets were in the section reserved for people who had "paid the bribe" of maintaining a Baylor Bear Foundation membership at a certain level.

And yet, here they were in our section. The enemy had infiltrated our ranks. Finally I turned to my dad, and with as much tact as a young child can have, I asked. *"How did we end up with THEM in our section???"*

The world of college football is a world of BIG plays, BIG emotions, BIG money and BIG rivalries. Identities are fixed by team colors, mascots and shared history. Nuance is non-existent. *We* are united in our oneness and in our opposition to *them*. Every Saturday there are clear stakes, clear sides, and all that matters is winning. When you step into the stadium, everything is a zero-sum game. In order for us to win, they must lose.

While these realities had never been shared with me, their truth was clear enough, so that even as a young child I "knew" that burnt orange and white did not belong in our section.

I was mystified when my dad began to share with me the identities of the people wearing burnt orange and white. They were doctors, lawyers, dentists and business people who lived and worked in Waco, but had gone to undergrad at the University of Texas. They were the same people that sat in our section every other week of the year. They supported

Baylor most Saturdays _and_ rooted for their alma-mater when Baylor played UT. They were not the enemy. They were our neighbors, friends, co-workers and members of our church.

This moment was an early introduction into the layered nature of our identities. Those people in different colored hats and jerseys were people too and, more importantly, people first. For me, this moment shrunk the distance between us and them.

As we continue in our lenten journey of saying 'Yes' after a year of 'No,' I believe Jesus is inviting us to a spiritual practice that also shrinks the distance between us and them: Praying... for our enemies.

In the Sermon on the Mount Jesus says:

"You have heard that it was said, You must love your neighbor and hate your enemy. But I say to you, love your enemies and pray for those who harass you so that you will be acting as children of your Father who is in heaven."

Matthew 5:43-45a

The Message paraphrases it this way.

"You're familiar with the old written law, 'Love your friend,' and its unwritten companion, 'Hate your enemy.' I'm challenging that. I'm telling you to love your enemies. Let them bring out the best in you, not the worst. When someone gives you a hard time, respond with the supple moves of prayer, for then you are working out of your true selves, your God-created selves."

Matthew 5:43-45a The Message

As I shared with my church family back at the beginning of the fall of 2020, I believe that our year of 'No' was a year of significant prayer. If there was a way to quantify the number of prayers said in a given year, I would expect 2020 to be one of the yearly leaders of the last half century.

2020 was a year of deep prayer. It was also a year of deepening divisions and widening gaps between us and them. The COVID-19 pandemic and our intentional actions to limit community spread have increased our isolation and decreased our face-to-face interactions with others. As Carey Nieuwhof notes: "As more of our life moves online, and as personal contact becomes less frequent, you and I get bolder and ruder {…} Distance between people desensitizes people. Generals have known this for a millennia. That's why soldiers wear uniforms and wear war paint. It not only identifies you, but it disguises your humanity. It's easier to shoot you when I can't see you {…} The same dynamic is at work in social media and our life online and any time we're not eyeball to eyeball in the room with another human."[18]

When we have greater distance between ourselves and others, it becomes easier for divisions to deepen, gaps to widen. It becomes easier to perceive that everyone who disagrees with us, even on a single thing, is

---

[18] https://careynieuwhof.com/pastors-heres-why-everyones-so-mad-at-you-right-now/

our enemy. And it becomes easier for us to hate those who we see as our enemy.

I believe that Jesus invites us to pray for our enemy because he knows that prayer is an act of radical intimacy that deeply connects us to God and to who God created us to be. It is an act that draws us closer to God and to those whom we pray for. It helps us see beyond the markers of our difference - the colors we wear, the teams we root for, the opinions we hold and the candidates we vote for. It helps us see the whites of each other's eyes, and our shared humanity.[19]

When we say 'Yes' to praying for our enemies, we are shrinking the gap between us and them, and in doing so saying 'Yes' to the new beginning Christ is bringing out of this year of 'No.'

---

[19] If music speaks to your soul, please listen to "See the Love" by *The Brilliance* this week. You can find it in all the places you like to listen to music.

MONDAY

"We love because God first loved us. Those who say, "I love God" and hate their brothers or sisters are liars. After all, those who don't love their brothers or sisters whom they have seen can hardly love God whom they have not seen!"
1 John 4:19-20

REFLECTION:

"Far from being the pious injunction of a utopian dreamer, this command [to love and pray for our enemies] is an absolute necessity for the survival of our civilization […] Because Jesus wasn't playing; because he was serious. We have the Christian and moral responsibility to seek to discover the meaning of these words, and to discover how we can live out this command, and why we should live by this command."[20]   *- Martin Luther King, Jr.*

---

20 https://kinginstitute.stanford.edu/king-papers/documents/loving-your-enemies-sermon-delivered-dexter-avenue-baptist-church

#SAYYESTODAY:

In his preaching on the call to love and pray for our enemy Martin Luther King Jr reminds us that "In order to love your enemies, you must begin by analyzing self." Today write down one person you think of as an enemy, and ask yourself the question, "What might I have done to bring out the pain, resentment, or hurt of this person?" Reflect on this for a moment, and as you do, pray to for the person whose name you've written down.

PRAYER:

Loving God, in these days of deepening divisions, reveal to me my role creating pain, hurt, or harm with _____. Forgive me for the ways in which I have failed, and show me how to better love _____.

Amen.

TUESDAY

"Instead, love your enemies, do good, and lend expecting nothing in return. If you do, you will have a great reward. You will be acting the way children of the Most High act, for He is kind to ungrateful and wicked people. Be compassionate just as your Father is compassionate"
Luke 6:35-36

REFLECTION:

"People really are wonderful. This does not mean that people cannot be awful and do real evil. They can. Yet as you begin to see with the eyes of God, you start to realize that people's anger and hatred and cruelty come from their own pain and suffering. As we begin to see their words and behavior as simply the acting out of their suffering, we can have compassion for them."[21]
- Archbishop Desmond Tutu

---

[21] Desmond Tutu, God Has a Dream, 97.

#SAYYESTODAY:

Spend five minutes engaging in a compassion meditation.[22]

1. Find a comfortable sitting position.

2. Take several deep breaths.

3. Silently say to yourself the following lines: May I be free from suffering. May I be well in body, mind, and heart. May I find peace and joy.

4. As you feel warmth coming from your heart, try to extend that feeling to someone you love very much- a relative, friend, or even a pet.

5. Remember when this person was having a difficult time. Notice what it feels like to experience their pain.

6. Silently repeat the following lines: May you be free from suffering. May you be well in body, mind, and heart. May you find peace and joy.

7. Think about someone with whom you have a difficult relationship.

---

[22] Dalai Lama and Desmond Tutu, The Book of Joy, 338-340. (Adapted)

8. Think about a time when they have endured suffering. Notice what it feels like to experience their pain.

9. Silently repeat the following lines: May you be free from suffering. May you be well in body, mind, and heart. May you find peace and joy.

10. Allow your feelings of compassion to fill your heart, and radiate this feeling of compassion out to the world.

PRAYER:

God of grace, you show me compassion and mercy, even when I am at my worst. Thank you for your love that knows no bounds. Give me your eyes to see others, even those who are hard to love, as your beloved sons and daughters. Help me to show compassion, as you show compassion towards me. In Jesus' name, **Amen**.

WEDNESDAY

"Bear with each other and forgive one another if any of you has a grievance against someone. Forgive as the Lord forgave you."
Colossians 3:13 NIV

REFLECTION:

"Now a new kindness
Seems to have entered time
And I can see how that hurt
Has schooled my heart
In a compassion I would
Otherwise have never learned."[23]

- John O'Donohue

---

[23] John O'Donohue, Benedictus, 187.

#SAYYESTODAY:

Light a candle and focus on it. Let this light come to represent the light of Christ; let this light wash over you with love. And then, when you're ready, close your eyes and see the person or persons with whom you have a grievance. As you see them, invite that candle's light to shine forth, sit with the image of the one(s) with whom you have a grievance, and allow the light of Christ to emanate forth from within this person. Spend at least three minutes here seeing the person(s) as someone who also contains the light of Christ. When you open your eyes, as the "amen" to your prayer, reflect on how you now feel in relation to this person(s). Can you bear with them a little easier? Have you learned something new about compassion? Are you ready to extend forgiveness?

PRAYER:

Holy Christ,

Forgiver of my sins, teach me of your compassion, of your light, of your love. Teach me how to soften so that I, too, may come to see you in each person I encounter. Teach me the fullness of mercy so that I might grow in my capacity to bear with the people of my life.

Amen.

THURSDAY

"Heal me, Lord, and I'll be healed.
Save me and I'll be saved,
for you are my heart's desire."
Jeremiah 17:14

REFLECTION:

"We each stand in need of healing, but in this ministry we recognise also the social dimension. The healing of divided communities and nations, and the healing of the earth itself, have their place alongside the healing of broken bodies, hurt minds and wounded hearts, and of the hurts and divisions within ourselves."[24]

---

[24] The Iona Community, Iona Abbey Worship Book, 109.

#SAYYESTODAY:

Have you ever noticed when you hold a grudge, when you stay mad, or envious, or withhold forgiveness, that you are the one that can become ill? Christ offers us salvation. From the word salvation, we also get our word salve, an ointment used to promote healing of the skin or as protection. When Christ offers us salvation, it is not just for our souls, but for our whole selves; this includes our relationships.

Sometimes the work of praying for our enemies begins with the work of praying for ourselves. Say 'Yes' today to do healing work for yourself. Identify a wound you have, then offer it in prayer to God. Ask God to show you the work to do in order to clean and put salve on the wound. Take this practice a step further today by calling a trusted friend, spouse, or mentor, and ask them to pray for you in this specific situation.

PRAYER:

Holy Christ,

You have been called the balm to the soul. Would you lay thick the salve of your salvation upon my wounds today? Would you teach me that the abundant life you offer is not fully realized until my whole self is made right with you – my soul, my mind, my body, and my relationships? Be like a mother who cleans her child's skinned knee so that in your care I might better understand salve and salvation.

Amen.

FRIDAY

"Bless people who harass you — bless and don't curse them."
Romans 12:14

REFLECTION:

"Bless them that persecute you. If our enemy cannot put up with us any longer and takes to cursing us, our immediate reaction must be to lift up our hands and bless him. Our enemies are the blessed of the Lord. Their curse can do us no harm. May their poverty be enriched with all the riches of God, with the blessing of Him whom they seek to oppose in vain. We are ready to endure their curses so long as they redound to their blessing."[25]   *- Deitrich Bonhoeffer*

#SAYYESTODAY:

Today re-read Romans 12:10-21. When you think about your enemy, those who have harmed you in some way, remember that they are a

---

[25] Deitrich Bonhoeffer, "The Enemy", The Cost of Discipleship, http://metapundit.net/sections/bonhoeffer/enemy

tainted image of the God who created them. They need your empathy and your prayers more than your condemnation.

Pray for them, that God softens their hearts, and they come to see the error of their ways.

PRAYER:

Creator God,

In the beginning you created humankind in your image. Ever since then, humankind has fallen short of living into your image, except for Jesus Christ.

Forgive me for the error of my ways; the times when I treat others as if they are my enemies.

Forgive my enemies, and show them the error of their ways, that they may find peace and joy in your presence!

Amen.

SATURDAY

"Jesus said, "Father, forgive them, for they don't know what they're doing."
Luke 23:34

REFLECTION:

"To forgive another person from the heart is an act of liberation. We set that person free from the negative bonds that exist between us. We say, 'I no longer hold your offense against you' But there is more. We also free ourselves from the burden of being the 'offended one.' As long as we do not forgive those who have wounded us, we carry them with us or, worse, pull them as a heavy load. The great temptation is to cling in anger to our enemies and then define ourselves as being offended and wounded by them. Forgiveness, therefore, liberates not only the other but also ourselves. It is the way to the freedom of the children of God."[26]
- Henri Nouwen

---

[26] Henri Nouwen, Bread for the Journey: A Daybook of Wisdom and Faith.

#SAYYESTODAY:

Jesus prayed, "Father forgive them" for the people who were crucifying him, as he was nailed to the cross. These words show God's willingness to forgive us of our sins, and they invite us to follow in his footsteps—to become a people who also pray, "Father forgive them, for they don't know what they're doing." Take a few moments to think about the people who have wronged you. Perhaps even write their names down. Reflect on this question: Am I willing to pray this prayer of Jesus?

PRAYER:

Father, forgive them, for they do not know what they are doing. You know their suffering and the pain they have caused me. Liberate me from the bonds of bitterness and resentment. Bring healing and peace to me ,and to those who have wronged me. In the name of the crucified One, **Amen**.

Saying 'Yes' to Reading the Bible... between the lines

Fourth Sunday of Lent

My mom was driving and I was in the passenger seat when, from the back seat, a question arose: "Do you know how cracks in the sidewalk get made?" The voice belonged to my then toddler of a sister--and my own childlike curiosity of a preteen was sparked. "No, how do the cracks in the sidewalk come to be?"

The answer, you see, was quite simple as my sister's voice, elated with the invitation, spilled the secrets to cracks in sidewalks. "Well, it's because at the center of the world there are dinosaurs, and when they get mad, they stomp around, and that causes cracks to form in our sidewalks." You see, simple.

Though my sister and mom have forgotten that particular childhood story, it's one that I have held onto. It's a story that invites wonder. It's a story that weaves together what my sister had learned about dinosaurs with a question she had about sidewalks. Her young wisdom is one that can teach us something about God and the Bible.

You see, I was recently standing in front of my book shelf. And there staring back at me was the Bible, but this particular Bible is broken out by each book of the Bible and leaves a blank page for journaling next to the text. As I stood there pondering which book of the Bible to pull off the shelf, I was underwhelmed. *"Well, I did a lot of work with the Prophets last year, and I feel like I've just read all the Gospels; Paul - no thanks, law books are just boring... everything else seems irrelevant for the time."* Each of the sixty-six books that make up the library of our Scriptures just felt bland and uninviting, let alone inspiring.

There was no dove descending on my head, no light breaking forth from behind the clouds, streaming through my window to illuminate a choice and no angelic proclamations.

Have you ever felt this way?

I found myself reminiscing about dinosaurs and sidewalks and wondering: *why on earth did that story pop into my head*? And in the ways minds can wander with no prompting or guidance, my mind then turned to another odd story, but one in the Bible. So, my hand reached out and pulled Genesis down from the shelf, and as I crossed my legs to root down into my big yellow chair in the corner of my office, my thumb flipped through chapters until it reached chapter thirty-two - the story of Jacob wrestling with God.

Do you remember the story? In it, Jacob is anxious about reuniting with his brother Esau because there's a lot of past family drama about birth rights and tricks, and Jacob was at the center of it all. Jacob, the ever-clever fox, tries to protect what is his by crossing the river in case his brother isn't really ready to forgive him like he says. Then, for some reason Jacob remained separate from his family and his belongings. It just says, "But Jacob stayed apart by himself, and a man wrestled with him until dawn broke." (Genesis 32:24). Yep, pretty weird. And it gets weirder, because as dawn is breaking, the man becomes desperate to be able to leave and Jacob agrees to let him go, but only if he'll bless Jacob. I haven't watched a lot of wrestling in my life, but I am unaware of any kind of blessings being part of the athletic feat of a wrestling match. The man, who, yes, we come to know was God, tears the tendon in Jacob's thigh so he'll limp for the rest of his life. But God also blesses Jacob. God changes Jacob's name to Israel or *the one who struggled with God and man and won.*

It's an odd story, and yet now my hand flies across the blank page, asking, wondering, *what in my life is already in the throes of a wrestling match?*

And there it is: *midrash,* or reading the Bible between the lines.

Midrash is a deep and very old Jewish practice. A tradition so beloved that I will not pretend that we will get to the heart of it all in this week-long practice, but we will dive into one piece of this beautiful practice. There are two forms of *midrash* -- *halacha* and *aggdah.* The practice we'll say "Yes" to together this Lent is the latter, *midrash aggdah.*

I make the distinction here between *halacha* and *aggdah,* or the two ways that one can practice *midrash,* because I wish for us to understand that the practice we're diving into is one that is ancient. It is a practice that has sacred roots, and I would be doing a disservice to the work of Jewish Rabbis and thinkers, if I were to pretend that in a week's time we'll cover it all. So know that though, yes, we'll specifically be practicing *midrash aggdah;* for the shorthand I'll primarily refer it as *midrash* going forward.

You might be thinking, dear reader, I just went from reading a cute story of childhood recollections to being kicked into the deep end with these heavy-lifting Hebraic terms, but bear with me just a short while longer. For I believe you'll discover you have already practiced *midrash* by reading this chapter and perhaps, have even already practiced *midrash* for yourself. *Midrash* means to search out; it is the act of looking for God in Scripture. *Midrash* invites us to explore what we do not know so that we may better come to know the one we desire to know. Judith Kunst, in her book *The Burning Word*, puts it this way:

"*Midrash* reads the Hebrew Bible not for what is familiar but for what is unfamiliar, not for what is clear, but what is unclear and then wrestles with the text passionately, playfully, and reverently. *Midrash* views the Bible as one side of a conversation started by God, containing an implicit invitation, even command to keep the conversation, argument, story, poem going."

So I wonder, dear reader, does any of this feel familiar? Have you, whether already knowing the word *midrash aggdah* or not, already practiced reading the Bible between the lines? Have you ever entered into the conversation? Or better yet, a wrestling match with God?

This week of Lent, we'll say 'Yes' to reading the Bible between the lines. We'll know that when we say 'Yes' to *midrash* we are also saying 'Yes' to:
- growing our own faith;
- being in awe of God;
- protecting the mystery of God;
- remembering that we serve a living God;
- being in a community of saints both living and in the cloud of witnesses;

• that it is our choice to search and be about the business of God on earth.

If you've ever found yourself staring blankly at the Bible, wondering what to read or if it's even worth picking up; if you've ever felt like your faith has just grown stale – then may you hear the whispers of the Holy Spirit saying 'Yes' this week. Dear reader, may you enter this week with the wisdom of a child, a fervently tenacious curiosity, and a willing spirit that would even dare to wrestle with God.

MONDAY

"Then he said, 'Your name won't be Jacob any longer, but Israel, because you struggled with God and with men and won.'"
Genesis 32:28

REFLECTION:

"[The Holy Spirit's] aim is to envelop and hide secret mysteries in ordinary words under the pretext of a narrative of some kind and of an account of visible things."[27]   *- Origen*

#SAYYESTODAY:

Today read Genesis 32:22-32. Then pray, asking the Holy Spirit to draw near this week to wrestle with you as you say 'Yes' to practicing the different facets of *midrash* (or reading the Bible between the lines).

---

[27] Origen, Origen An Exhortation to Martyrdom, Prayer and Selected Works, 187.

97

PRAYER:

Holy Spirit Come!

May your Spirit's hovering over the chaos of my soul alight in me. Where there is ambivalence, invite stirring; where there is avoidance, invite challenge. May the sweat of my brow spent furrowed in wondering and pondering result in new depths of love for who you are and who you invite me to be.

Amen.

TUESDAY

"Allow the children to come to me," Jesus said. "Don't forbid them, because the kingdom of heaven belongs to people like these children."
Matthew 19:14

REFLECTION:

"When medieval map makers came to the limit of their knowledge of the known world, they ofttimes wrote in the empty space, 'Here be dragons.' There is something frightening about moving into the unknown, which might harm or devour us."[28]   *- Elizabeth A. Johnson*

#SAYYESTODAY:

Today, read a story with a child, whether it's your own child or FaceTiming with a dear friend's or relative's child. Pick out a story to read together. Then after the story is over, ask the child to tell you what they

---

[28] Elizabeth A. Johnson, Quest for the Living God, 5.

think happened after the story ended. Observe how easy it often is for children to step right into the practice of midrash, like stepping off the drawn lines of a map into dragon territory. Listen to their delight, their unleashed curiosity. When the storytelling is finished, thank the child for his or her sharing.

PRAYER:

Holy Spirit,

May we throw off the piety and rituals of adulthood that would bar us from knowing you with a child's wonder, curiosity, playfulness, and delight. May we dare to go off the known map so that we might, in the unknown, encounter the One worth knowing more.

Amen.

WEDNESDAY

"But Jonah thought this was utterly wrong, and he became angry."
Jonah 4:1

REFLECTION:

"I noted that it is sometimes hard to tell whether you are being killed or saved by the hands that turn your life upside down."[29]
- Barbara Brown Taylor

#SAYYESTODAY:

Many followers of God have had their lives turned upside down. Jonah, perhaps, is the most classic example of this. Have you ever noticed that the book of Jonah just ends-- abruptly? Read Jonah 4:1-11 today, then engage in "wonder statements." Wondering statements are a practice that

---

[29] Barbara Brown Taylor, Learning to Walk in the Dark, 67.

help pull the reader between the lines of a story to see where perhaps, the Holy Spirit is waiting between the story and your life. These statements are simple, are often questions, and usually begin with "I wonder..." An example might be, "I wonder how long it took Jonah to come down from the hill?" Try writing down at least five "wonder statements," and then end by examining what you've written: Have you revealed something about God? Yourself? Your community? Many have said that Jonah's final chapter is like holding up a mirror – what do you see in the mirror?

PRAYER:

Holy Spirit,

Help my mind to *wonder* as it *wanders* through the lines of a familiar story. Spark questions in the deep knowing place of my soul so that I might see where you, Jonah, and I meet here today.

Amen.

THURSDAY

"Jesus replied, 'What is written in the Law? How do you interpret it?'"
Luke 10:26

REFLECTION:

"It is haunting work to recall the sins of our past. But is this not the work we have been called to anyway? Is this not the work of the Holy Spirit to illuminate truth and inspire transformation? It's haunting. But it's also holy."[30]
- Austin Channing Brown

#SAYYESTODAY:

Read Luke 10:25-37. As you encounter what will likely be very familiar passages of Scripture, try to suspend what you've read or learned about it previously. Do this gently. Your greatest aide for this is to read the passage and be filled with curiosity. Ask questions of the text. Write them down, if

---

[30] Austin Channing Brown, I'm Still Here: Black Dignity in a World Made for Whiteness, 118.

that is useful to you. Do not judge your questions – simply allow them to rise to the surface. Questions invite us between and beyond the story into the haunting and holy work of transformation.

PRAYER:

Holy Spirit,

If Christ is my template for an abundant life, then may I too be filled to the brim with good questions. Let my questions spur others around me deeper in their thoughts, or help me to see your constant new life even in the most familiar of stories. May the questions you arise in my soul dare me to the deeper care of neighbor that I have overlooked, greater love that speaks boldly, and unwavering eyes from seeing the truth I have overshadowed in quaint platitudes about familiar stories.

Amen.

FRIDAY

"When the time came, Jesus took his place at the table, and the apostles joined him."
Luke 22:14

REFLECTION:

"One night a year we tell each other the great stories of our faith so that we can remember who we are. Once a year we gather around the fire of a beautifully imperfect candle and tell each other about God and God's people."[31]
- Nadia Bolz-Weber

#SAYYESTODAY:

Gather your community, your people. Get them together online or in person, and spend some time sharing the important stories. Listen for where God shows up beyond the words shared in the time together;

---

[31] Nadia Bolz-Weber, Accidental Saints: Finding God in All the Wrong People, 147.

perhaps it'll be in an emotion, a thought, a good question. Notice how God is still showing up in God's people today.

PRAYER:

Holy Spirit,

Show up in my gathering spaces, those places where it is easier to reach past ink and lines to dive deep into the marrow of life. Show me where I have overlooked God when I get caught in the daily to-dos, so that I might find more ta-das. Reveal Christ on earth in the storytellers who reveal you as the one woven into the very fabric of each moment.

Amen.

SATURDAY

"Jesus looked at him carefully and loved him. He said, 'You are lacking one thing. Go, sell what you own, and give the money to the poor. Then you will have treasure in heaven. And come, follow me.'"
Mark 10:21

REFLECTION:

"…and the most common temptation of all for us is to use belonging to the right group and practicing its proper rituals as a substitute for any personal or life-changing encounter with the Divine."[32]   *- Richard Rohr*

#SAYYESTODAY:

Reflect on a moment in your life where you felt close to God, whether through church rituals, getting lost in nature, or even at home with your family. Spend some time remembering the story and then tell yourself the

---

[32] Richard Rohr, Eager to Love, 5.

story. As you tell this holy story to yourself, use any of the *midrash* practices you've engaged in this week: invite the Holy Spirit's presence, approach your story with new curiosity, create wonder statements, ask questions, or invite a close friend to listen to the story with you. After the story has been told, step back and look at what your *midrashing* of this personal story has revealed about God.

PRAYER:

Beloved Spirit,

May I endeavor for the Holy Scriptures to come alive in my life. May your challenge, wrestling, and hiding in between the lines of holy texts reveal to me that you are also challenging, wrestling, and hiding in between the moments of my very life. May *midrash* become a reminder that you are ever-living and ever-lasting, and that you offer the same fullness to me.

Amen.

SAYING 'YES' TO RESTORING...
RELATIONSHIPS WITH OTHERS

FIFTH SUNDAY OF LENT

Shortly after the hearse drove away, and the other cars had left the parking lot, she walked back into the sanctuary and picked up a modest flower arrangement that had been left behind.

A few moments earlier, she was seated with her sister and brothers weeping together over the loss of their father. The stories they told during the service brought laughter and tears as they stirred up memories of years gone by, and the special times they had shared together as a family.

After the service was over they, all agreed to meet for lunch at Farina's. They have a great room in the back where the family could visit, share more memories, and say all the things they couldn't say during the eulogy. But she was running behind.

I asked her, "Are you meeting the others for lunch?"

"No," she said with a defeated look on her face, "I'm the black sheep of the family."

I didn't ask why, nor did she seem to want to talk about it, but it was clear that her father's death wasn't the first death she had experienced in her family. The relationships she once shared with them had been dead for quite some time. And she clearly grieved the loss of those relationships, almost as much as she did the loss of her father.

The story is all too familiar. One or more members of the family are ostracized and excluded from shared time because of something, or some things, that had happened in the past. Something that drove a wedge between them and the others. Friends who were once inseparable, who comforted, supported, and celebrated life's highs and lows with one another haven't spoken in years. Folks who used to sit on the front porch and wave to their neighbors as they drove by don't wave anymore.

Perhaps it was something that was said or done in the heat of the moment. Perhaps it was something overlooked that should have been noticed. Perhaps it was simply time getting away from us. Whatever the case, relationships that were once loving, intimate, and important in our lives fall apart or away and are in need of restoration.

In a year filled with the loneliness and isolation of 'No,' God offers the comfort and companionship of 'Yes.' 'Yes' to Restoring…relationships with others.

In a letter written to the people in the Corinthian church, the apostle Paul reminds us that God is a God of restoration and reconciliation.

"So then, if anyone is in Christ, that person is part of the new creation. The old things have gone away, and look, new things have arrived! All of these new things are from God, who reconciled us to himself through Christ and who gave us the ministry of reconciliation. In other words, God was reconciling the world to himself through Christ, by not counting people's sins against them. He has trusted us with this message of reconciliation. So we are ambassadors who represent Christ. God is negotiating with you through us. We beg you as Christ's representatives, "Be reconciled to God!" God caused the one who didn't know sin to be sin for our sake so that through him we could become the righteousness of God."

2 Corinthians 5:17-21

Paul wrote, "… if anyone is in Christ, that person is part of the new creation." If we're not familiar with the original creation story, these words cause us to pause and ask, "Why is there a need for 'the new creation'? What went wrong with the old one?"

If we go back to the original creation story in Genesis we find that God created humankind to be in relationships.

"God spoke: 'Let us make human beings in our image, make them reflecting our nature…God created human beings; he created them godlike, Reflecting God's nature. He created them male and female. "

Genesis 1:26a, 27, *The Message*

"Then the LORD God said, "It's not good that the human is alone…"

Genesis 2:18

In Genesis 3, scripture tells us that sin was introduced to human beings and, in choosing sin, human beings separated themselves from God.

"During that day's cool evening breeze, they heard the sound of the LORD God walking in the garden; and the man and his wife hid themselves from the LORD God in the middle of the garden's trees."

Genesis 3:8

At the heart of Paul's message is the fact that God, in Christ, would do anything, up to and including die, to restore God's relationship with God's people. There's nothing God wouldn't do to reconcile with God's children.

These verses fall under the heading "Ministry of Reconciliation," in the Common English Bible.

If we were created in God's image then, in our new creation, we must desire restoration of relationships like God does. If we are "ambassadors who represent Christ," then we would do everything we could to restore the relationships we've lost; whether it be our doing or something the other person has done.

In 2020 we had to say 'No' to many things, including fellowship with family, friends, and neighbors, and this has left us feeling isolated and lonely. Some of those relationships have been severed due to differences in political ideology or some other disagreement or transgression.

In saying 'Yes' to restoring relationships with others, we are offering comfort and companionship to a world that feels lonely and isolated. We are also living into the very nature of God in whom we were created.

MONDAY

"Because everyone will die for their own sins: whoever eats sour grapes will have a bitter taste in their own mouths."
Jeremiah 31:30

REFLECTION:

"Do not give your attention to what others do or fail to do; give it to what you do or fail to do."[33]   - *Buddha*

#SAYYESTODAY:

Today read Jeremiah 31:23-33. Then pray, asking God what your role was in the severing of the relationship you wish to restore. Resist dwelling on their transgressions in order to fully focus on your own.

---

[33] Buddha, https://www.goodreads.com/quotes/tag/self-responsibility

PRAYER:

God of Light,

Open my eyes to see where I have erred, offended, or harmed my sister, my brother. Soften my war-torn and hardened heart that I may know my role in the separation.

Help me understand where I have contributed to the distance that separates us, so that I may address that which is in me.

Amen.

TUESDAY

"What is the source of conflict among you? What is the source of your disputes? Don't they come from your cravings that are at war in your own lives?"
James 4:1

REFLECTION:

"Evaluation eliminates frustration. We should evaluate unrealistic expectations. Unrealistic expectations become unmet expectations. And unmet expectations are like kindling wood – it only takes but a spark of frustration to set them ablaze and burn those involved."[34]
- Lysa TerKeurst

---

[34] Lysa TerKeurst, The Best Yes, p.35.

#SAYYESTODAY:

Today read James 4:1-12. Then reflect on whether your relationship has suffered because of some unmet expectation; whether it be their unmet expectation of you or your unmet expectation of them.

PRAYER:

Sovereign God,

Forgive me when I assume the role of judge and jury.

Open my eyes to the times I place the burden of my expectations on others and hold them accountable to my laws, oftentimes without even communicating them.

Remind me that your expectations alone ought to be our desire.

Amen.

WEDNESDAY

"Be tolerant with each other and, if someone has a complaint against anyone, forgive each other. As the Lord forgave you, so also forgive each other."
Colossians 3:13

REFLECTION:

"It's the hardest thing to give away
And the last thing on your mind today
It always goes to those who don't deserve

It's the opposite of how you feel
When the pain they caused is just too real
Takes everything you have just to say the word...

Forgiveness...Forgiveness...

It'll clear the bitterness away
It can even set the prisoner free

There is no end to what its power can do

So, let it go and be amazed
By what you see through eyes of grace
The prisoner that it really frees is you

Forgiveness…Forgiveness"[35]   *- Matthew West*

#SAYYESTODAY:

Today read Colossians 3:1-15. Then think about the times you have fallen short of being Christlike, being the person God wills you to be. Perhaps this posture will soften your heart to forgive as you've been forgiven.

---

[35] Matthew West, Forgiveness, https://www.azlyrics.com/lyrics/matthewwest/forgiveness.html

PRAYER:

Lord God,

I have fallen short of your expectations. I have sinned against you and others.

Yet, in your great love, you offer forgiveness for those who confess and repent. As I face your cross, forgive my transgressions and cleanse me.

Help me, O God, to follow your lead and to forgive those who have transgressed against me.

Amen.

THURSDAY

"Love each other like the members of your family. Be the best at showing honor to each other."
Romans 12:10

REFLECTION:

"Reaching out to others washes away years of questions and regret."[36]
- Catie Kovelman

#SAYYESTODAY:

Today read Romans 12:10-21. Ask yourself, "Who do I miss the most that I haven't spoken to in a while?" Then, regardless of the reason you haven't spoken, pick up the phone and call them. If they are in need of

---

[36] Catie Kovelman, "Why You Should Reconnect With Old Friends While Social Distancing", https://www.readunwritten.com/2020/03/30/why-reconnect-old-friends-social-distancing/,

forgiveness, offer it. If you are in need of forgiveness, ask for it. If you just haven't spoken in a while just say, "I've missed you!"

PRAYER:

God of Love,

Thank you for the people you have brought into my life; for the friendships, the family, and the acquaintances of the past, present and future. They have given me great joy and have shown me how to love and how you love.

Give me the courage to reach beyond my doubt and to call the one you have placed on my heart!

Amen.

FRIDAY

"God so loved the world that he gave his only Son, so that everyone who believes in him won't perish but will have eternal life."
John 3:16

"This is how we know love: Jesus laid down his life for us, and we ought to lay down our lives for our brothers and sisters."
1 John 3:16

REFLECTION:

"Well, I've sacrificed time with family and friends
Gave up vacations for work without end
Twenty four seven, three hundred and sixty five
But was willing to make the sacrifice

But empty or full, I've carried my pail
You don't drink the water if you don't dig the well
Through blood sweat and tears I have built a good life
But it didn't come without sacrifice

But I was gonna be rich no matter how much it cost
And I was gonna win no matter how much I lost
All through the years I kept my eye on the prize
You ask if it's worth the sacrifice, the sacrifice

I think about Jesus and all that he gave
And the ultimate sacrifice that he made
He is my strength and my guiding light
And he's taught me that nothing's without sacrifice"[37]
- Dolly Parton

#SAYYESTODAY:

Today read 1 John 3:16-24. Reflect on your most intimate and personal relationships, and think about what makes them different than the others. Relationships naturally grow deeper the more we are willing to sacrifice for the other.

---

[37] Dolly Parton, The Sacrifice, https://www.lyrics.com/lyric/27454307/Dolly+Parton/The+Sacrifice,

Then do something completely self-sacrificial for someone.   Send flowers to your spouse.   Send a handwritten note to a family member. Have a meal unexpectedly delivered to a friend.

PRAYER:

God of Grace,

In Christ you gave me the example of self-sacrificial love.   Though I did nothing to deserve it, you gave your all so that I may have life in abundance!

Give me the heart to follow your lead. Give me a heart of generosity and kindness that someone may experience your love through me today!

Amen.

SATURDAY

"So then, if anyone is in Christ, that person is part of the new creation. The old things have gone away, and look, new things have arrived! All of these new things are from God, who reconciled us to himself through Christ and who gave us the ministry of reconciliation."
2 Corinthians 5:17-18

REFLECTION:

"We can't change the person we're estranged from, but God can. Even when the door seems firmly closed, God is able to open it. Do all you can to restore that broken relationship — and trust God for the outcome."[38]
- Billy Graham

---

38 Billy Graham, Rebuilding Relationships, https://www.faithgateway.com/rebuilding-relationships/#.YAH78OIKjGl

#SAYYESTODAY:

Today re-read 1 Corinthians 5:17-21. Then pray that God's Holy Spirit will give you the patience and peace to trust that God will live into God's promise of restoration and reconciliation.

PRAYER:

Lord Jesus,

I give you thanks, for you have made all things, and in you, all things hold together.

Through your blood, you have brought reconciliation and restoration between humankind and God, and you have given us the same ministry of reconciliation.

Remind me that no relationship is beyond your healing power. But that you restore relationships in your way, in your time, and for your purpose.

Grant me the patience and trust to do what I can and to leave the rest to you. **Amen.**

Restoring... relationships with others

SAYING 'YES' TO ENTERING THE STORY

HOLY WEEK - PALM SUNDAY

As you look around, you see it.

The airborne greenery aiming for eyeballs...

The harried parents desperate to have this turn out "just right"...

The dressed-up kids, both confused and overjoyed that *this* is the day that they get to be loud and active in worship...

The organized chaos that kid's ministry directors and volunteers have spent weeks trying to plan...

The tickled grandparents secretly hoping that the train runs off the tracks...

Yes. You've guessed it. We've made it to Palm Sunday - the day when all of the pent-up energy and penitence of Lent comes to a head in the beautiful chaos, loud Hosannas, and aggressively waived palms that begin worship.

What a spectacle. What a sight to behold. What a moment.

As I think about this moment, I wonder when was the last time you waved palms on Palm Sunday? At what point did you cede the kid wrangling, palm passing, and cat herding of the Palm Sunday processional to another generation of unsuspecting parents?

When Palm Sunday 2020 came around, it had been a number of years since I had braved the storm. While my kids were still young, I had begun leaving the palm processional to our kid's ministry team and my fellow parents. Perched high on the chancel, I assumed the prized role of an honorary tickled grandparent, and I liked it.

Palm Sunday 2020 changed that reality for me. It was the Palm Sunday of 'No.'

Gone was the full sanctuary.

Gone were the kids.

Gone were the palms.

Gone was the joyful chaos.

Gone were the people who delighted in the holy chaos with me.

As I experienced that Palm Sunday, I missed the cries of Hosanna. I missed Jesus and a bunch of kids parading us all into Holy Week. As I sat in my grief in this disrupted Palm Sunday, I felt a deep longing to jump back into the parade. I felt invited to cede my place as amused observer of cute children, and to say 'Yes' to entering the story of Holy Week with my whole being.

While we don't know exactly how Palm Sunday might be different this year as the COVID-19 pandemic continues, I do know that I'm saying 'Yes' to fully entering the story of Holy Week. Will you join me?

Today I invite you to begin entering the story of Holy Week by reading John 12:12-19.

DH

HOLY MONDAY

"Then Mary took an extraordinary amount, almost three-quarters of a pound, of very expensive perfume made of pure nard. She anointed Jesus' feet with it, then wiped his feet dry with her hair. The house was filled with the aroma of the perfume."
John 12:3

REFLECTION:

"So it is ourselves that we must spread under Christ's feet, not coats or lifeless branches or shoots of trees, matter which wastes away and delights the eye only for a few brief hours. But we have clothed ourselves with Christ's grace, with the whole Christ - 'for as many of you as were baptized into Christ have put on Christ' - so let us spread ourselves like coats under his feet"[39]
- Andrew of Crete

---

[39] Andrew of Crete, Bread and Wine: Readings for Lent and Easter, 30.

#SAYYESTODAY:

Holy Week is a week in which we encounter the sacrifice of Jesus for the world. In John 12, we also see Mary's act of deep sacrifice for Christ. Today read John 12:1-11. Then ask, "what gift can you give to God this Holy Week?"

PRAYER:

Sacrificial God,

Thank you for all of the ways in which your sacrificial love has been shown to me. As I enter this Holy Week, reveal to me how I can sacrifice for you.

Amen.

HOLY TUESDAY

"I assure you that unless a grain of wheat falls into the earth and dies, it can only be a single seed. But if it dies, it bears much fruit. Those who love their lives will lose them, and those who hate their lives in this world will keep them forever. Whoever serves me must follow me. Wherever I am, there my servant will also be. My Father will honor whoever serves me."
John 12:24-26

REFLECTION:

"I love him, I love him, I love him
And where he goes I'll follow, I'll follow, I'll follow

I will follow him, follow him wherever he may go
There isn't an ocean too deep
A mountain so high it can keep me away

I must follow him (follow him), ever since he touched my hand I knew
That near him I always must be

And nothing can keep him from me
He is my destiny (destiny)

I love him, I love him, I love him
And where he goes I'll follow, I'll follow, I'll follow
He'll always be my true love, my true love, my true love
From now until forever, forever, forever"[40]   *- Peggy March*

#SAYYESTODAY:

Today read John 12:24-33. Ask yourself, "How far down this road will I follow him until the cost is just too high? How far am I willing to go?" Then pray for strength to go the distance!

---

[40] Peggy March, "I Will Follow Him", https://genius.com/Peggy-march-i-will-follow-him-lyrics

PRAYER:

Lord Jesus,

The steps you took that led you to the cross are the steps that brought salvation to humankind. Words fall short of my gratitude and appreciation.

I choose to follow you, to be a disciple, to offer my life in service to you that I may find the eternal abundant life you have in store for me.

Grant me strength, courage, and perseverance that, through your Holy Spirit, I can run the race set before me and cross the finish line into your glory.

Amen.

HOLY WEDNESDAY

"After he said these things, Jesus was deeply disturbed and testified, 'I assure you, one of you will betray me.'"
John 13:21

REFLECTION:

"So then, with endurance, let's also run the race that is laid out in front of us, since we have such a great cloud of witnesses surrounding us. Let's throw off any extra baggage, get rid of the sin that trips us up, and fix our eyes on Jesus, faith's pioneer and perfecter. He endured the cross, ignoring the shame, for the sake of the joy that was laid out in front of him, and sat down at the right side of God's throne."   *Hebrews 12:1-2*

#SAYYESTODAY:

Today read John 13:21-32 and Luke 22:14-23. Take note of how, even when Jesus knows his betrayer is with him, he is still welcome at the table.   He is offered bread and cup - symbols of the sacrificial love of Jesus.

This Holy Week we come to the table with baggage.   We come with history. We come with failings from a long year unlike any we've known and from a lifetime of imperfect trying.   Sometimes this baggage can weigh us down and make us wonder if we are welcome at God's table.

I invite you today to "throw off any extra baggage, get rid of the sin that trips us up, and fix our eyes on Jesus, faith's pioneer and perfecter," as Hebrews so beautifully reminds us.

Write down on a piece of paper one piece of baggage you need to throw off.   Look at it one final time, release its weight on your soul and burn it.

PRAYER:

Holy Christ,

You are faith's pioneer and perfecter.   Today I give to you my extra baggage - the brokenness that holds me back, and I pray that you would help me to fix my eyes upon you today.

Amen.

MAUNDY THURSDAY

"I give you a new commandment: Love each other. Just as I have loved you, so you must also love each other. This is how everyone will know that you are my disciples, when you love each other."
John 13:34-35

REFLECTION:

"Then he poured water into a basin and began to wash the disciples' feet and to wipe them with the towel that was tied around him."   *John 13:5*

"As if you could stop this blessing from washing over you...as if you could change the course by which this blessing flows...as if you could control how it pours over you—unbidden, unsought, unasked, yet startling in the way it matches the need you did not know you had..."[41]   *- Jan Richardson*

---

[41] Jan Richardson, Circle of Grace, 2015, p.131-132.

#SAYYESTODAY:

Together we have journeyed through the season of Lent, reflecting on saying 'Yes' to reading the Bible, to praying for our enemies, to restoring relationships, to embracing Sabbath and healing, and to engaging in spiritual practices. This past Sunday, we celebrated Palm Sunday and Jesus, astride a young colt, being welcomed into Jerusalem by a crowd waving palm branches, rejoicing, and shouting, "Hosanna! Blessings on the one who comes in the name of the Lord! Blessings on the King of Israel!" (John 12:12-13)

As we read through John's account of this week leading up to Jesus' betrayal, trial, and crucifixion, it seems that the mood has shifted. On this evening, Jesus gathered with his disciples to observe the Passover meal. He knew what was ahead for him, and he was deeply troubled. In John 13, Jesus washed the feet of his disciples, announced that there was one among them who would betray him, prepared them for his death, and gave his disciples a new commandment, a mandate, to love one another as he loved them.

On this night of foot washing, last supper, fellowship, betrayal and new commandment, you are invited to read John 13:1-35. (You may also want to read from Matthew 26:17-30, Mark 14:12-26, or Luke 22:7-23.)

I wonder what it was like to have been with Jesus and his disciples that evening. I wonder how I would have responded to Jesus washing my feet or learning, as I sat around the table with my fellow disciples, that someone in the room was to betray Jesus.

As you read through this passage, what questions do you have?

What emotions do you experience?

What symbolism do you recognize in the foot washing, in the meal, and in the betrayal?

That evening, Jesus gave his disciples a new commandment. As people who claim to be Christians, how are we showing our love for each other so that people will know that we are followers of Jesus?

What do you hear God saying to you through this Maundy Thursday reading?

PRAYER:

Lord Jesus, on this night you were betrayed, you shared a meal with your closest friends and gave them a new commandment—to love each other as you love them. Walk with us in our times of doubt, betrayal, denial, and fear. Walk with us in our times of belief, faithfulness, admission, and courage. Teach us to love as you have commanded us to love, and to serve you faithfully all our days. Bless us in our times of trial and in our times of rejoicing. What a wondrous love you offer each of us.

Amen.

GOOD FRIDAY

"But Jesus let out a loud cry and died."
Mark 15:37

REFLECTION:

"But I don't want ice cream, I want a world where there is no need for pediatric oncology, UNICEF, military budgets, or suicide rails on the top floors of tall buildings. The world would drip with mercy. Thy kingdom come, I pray, and my heart aches. And my tongue trips over the rest. Thy will be done."[42]
- Kate Bowler

#SAYYESTODAY:

Imagine before you a great desert… and as you wander through the desert, you come to a great chasm. Its yawning expanse makes its way down to the darkest of depths. And there, sitting perched with feet

---

[42] Kate Bowler, Everything Happens for a Reason: And Other Lies I've Loved,151.

dangling over the ledge, is a man of Middle Eastern descent who turns slightly, revealing a glint of mischief in his eye and the tugging of his lip forming a half smile. The tilt of his head beckons you, in the smallest of movements to take the biggest step – the step to join him on the ledge.

It is an absolute travesty, in my clearly-not-dramatic-at-all opinion, that the Apostle's Creed contains an asterisk guiding the reader's eye down to the stricken line, "He descended into hell." We no longer say this line in a communal space, and our theology suffers for it. Instead of knowing where Christ was after his death, cute queries get asked, "Do you think Jesus took a really long nap?" or "Was Jesus already having a pre-party in heaven?" NO!

Jesus' death on the cross isn't the end of the pain. Jesus' love for us meant that he literally went to hell. Now I know the temptation on this day is to jump to the end of the story, to comfort ourselves with the knowledge of the happily ever after. But when we do, we ask cute questions in place of real questions, and we skip the fullness of Good Friday. We miss out on the vast beauty of Holy Week, and we miss an opportunity to be *good news*.

Because here is our reality; we as a world have lived through a pandemic and in its wake, we know the stories of loved ones dying alone, stories of spouses missing funerals because they were still COVID positive when their spouse died, stories of...I'll let you fill in your own. In the year 2021 we are still dealing with the impacts of last year – we are a world, a people, individuals in need of permission to grieve.

Good Friday is the day we sit with our feet dangling over the ledge into the chasm of death, and we dream of a world where COVID-19 never existed; we dream of a world where the military isn't needed; where children aren't diagnosed with horrid diseases. We dream and we allow our hearts to break knowing that these aren't so. And when we give ourselves the permission to mourn and to grieve, we will find that Christ is sitting right beside us, feet dangling over the ledge, too.

Today, read Mark's account of Christ's death (Mark 15:31-41). And then allow yourself to go sit on the ledge with the Savior who didn't just die for you, but went through hell for you. Allow yourself to acknowledge where you, too, have lived through hell, and where you need permission to mourn. Mourners, grievers, dreamers; you are welcome here on this Good Friday.

PRAYER:

Mischievous Christ,

Who overturned tables and expectations, in your death you showed us that pain and grief are welcome in your presence; for you too endured them. Today help me not to jump to the end of the story, but let me sit here with questions, with pain, and with you. Allow me to soak in the full presence of today, so that after this Good Friday I will never question if you have forsaken me.

Amen.

HOLY SATURDAY

The day before they watched Jesus die. On that day, the world as they knew it changed forever. On that day, the sight of their Rabbi, beaten and bloodied on the cross, was an image that would be etched into their memory for the rest of their lives. On that day, the wailing of the women was piercing to the heart. On that day, all their dreams—dreams of sight being restored to the blind, the liberation of the oppressed, and a new kingdom coming—were dashed right in front of them. It felt like someone knocked the wind out of them. The disciples ended Friday terrified and traumatized.

Then came Saturday. The Sabbath. The day to rest and be revived in God. Scripture has very little to say about the Saturday after Jesus' death. It seems that the world entered into a state of silence, where there were no words left to speak. Since it was Sabbath, the world was forced to pause and reflect on the aftermath of the crucifixion. The reality of recent events began to sink in. Where the pages of Scripture are silent, we are left wondering what precisely the disciples did on this day. Did they gather together, sharing stories of their beloved teacher, finding comfort in their shared grief? Did they sit by the shore of the sea of Galilee in silence, tears rolling down their faces, as they gazed upon those memory-laden waters? Or did they stay separated, each in their own homes, curled up in bed, crying to God in anguish?

On this particular day of rest, the disciples began to process the pain they bore. They were forced to sit with the emotions they felt. It was a liminal space, an in-between time.

We too are living in a liminal space, between "what was" and "what's next." Our life before March 2020 is now gone, and our life will never be the same. While there is a light at the end of the tunnel with vaccines, we are all still in the midst of a raging pandemic. Perhaps you might be living in a different sort of liminal space right now- through an empty nest, a health diagnosis, a job loss, a death of a loved one, a divorce, or a recent move.

Franciscan priest Richard Rohr writes that this liminal space is "where we are betwixt and between the familiar and the completely unknown. There alone is our old world left behind, while we are not yet sure of the new existence. That's a good space where genuine newness can begin."[43] Rohr reminds us of the importance of standing in the gap between "what was" and "what's next" because it creates space for transformation to begin. And as Barbara Brown Taylor so eloquently points out, "New life starts in the dark. Whether it is a seed in the ground, a baby in a womb, or Jesus in the tomb, it starts in the dark."[44] New life begins in that dark, liminal space.

---

[43] Richard Rohr, Everything Belongs: The Gift of Contemplative Prayer, 155.

[44] Barbara Brown Taylor, Learning to Walk in the Dark, 129.

Unlike the disciples on that Saturday after Jesus' crucifixion, we know that Jesus' death is not the end of the story. We know that the transformation of all things was already underway, and resurrection was just a day away. This is a hope that we can cling to in the midst of the liminal space we are living in now. In Isaiah 43:19, God promises, "Look! I'm doing a new thing; now it sprouts up; don't you recognize it?"

May you #sayyestoday to the in-between time of Holy Saturday. May you sit with the grief of Good Friday, while never losing sight of the promise of Easter Sunday. May you stand in the gap, waiting, watching, and preparing for the new thing God is doing and inviting you into.

PRAYER:

Dear God, as I sit betwixt and between "what was" and "what's next," help me to be fully present to this moment and all you offer me in it. Help me to enter the story of Holy Saturday, to stand in that liminal space alongside the first disciples. In the silence, in the grief, in the uncertainty, and in the possibilities of this liminal space, give me the grace to wait and to prepare for the new thing you are doing in me and in our world. In Jesus' name, **Amen.**

EASTER EPILOGUE

As I stood there with the wind whipping at my back and a chill in the air, I began to wonder if the sun was ever going to come up.

It was early in the morning on an Easter Sunday. It was one of those Easter Sundays that - because a of quirk of the calendar - was particularly early in the Spring. I was gathered lakeside with people from our church and community ready to celebrate the resurrection of Jesus. Ready to re-live that early morning moment in that ancient garden when the light of God's love began to radiate anew, showing that even in the darkest night, morning is coming.

We were ready… but it seemed like the sun was not.

This was my first Easter Sunday in a new community that I was pastoring, and this was the first Easter Sunrise service our community had had in many years. As odd as it may sound, I was feeling pressure: pressure for everything to work out; pressure for this new service, that had been my idea, to be meaningful and holy, and pressure to show that the new preacher wasn't going to butcher Easter.

I was feeling the pressure, and the sun was not cooperating.

As we sang the songs of Easter morning, my mind spun with the worry that we'd have to celebrate the Son-rise without the sunrise.

When we finished singing, I stepped up to lead us in prayer, and as we bowed our heads, it was dark. I prayed, hoping that the truth of Easter might be real to us. I prayed, asking that we might be able to lay aside our worries and fully enter the story. I prayed, longing for the glory of Easter to smack us in the head so clearly that even in our thickest moments we could see.

When we bowed our heads to pray, it was dark.

But when we opened our eyes, *light had come*!

As we experience this Easter after a year of 'No' I know it would be easy to see the darkness that abounds. Today I pray that the truth of Easter is clear to us. I pray that our journey of Saying 'Yes' has opened us to the new beginning that Christ is bringing out of this year of 'No.' I pray that we might see that even in the darkest night, morning is coming. **Amen**.

ABOUT THE CONTRIBUTORS:

Daniel Hawkins is the Lead Pastor of First United Methodist Cleburne. He lives in Texas with his wife, April, and three daughters Abby, Chloe and Harper. Connect with him on social media @DanielKHawkins and hear him on the Gather Grow Go Podcast.

Melissa Turkett is the Pastor of Community at First United Methodist Cleburne. You can keep up with her wanderings on www.melissaturkett.com or on Instagram @revmelissaturkett. She is a cohost of the Gather Grow Go podcast. Melissa lives in Texas with her husband, Patrick.

Katie Newkirk is the Associate Pastor at First United Methodist Church of Colleyville, with theological training at Texas Christian University and Southern Methodist University. Her ideal Sabbath involves spending time outdoors, journaling, and dinner and deep conversation with her husband, Christopher.

Meg Witmer-Faile is the Associate Director of the Center for Evangelism, Mission & Church Growth in the UMC's Central Texas Conference. Collaborating with congregations on New Faith Communities, Adaptive Leadership & Church Growth, First Impressions Hospitality and Coach Training workshops, she welcomes innovation, creativity, and conversations on diverse topics and worldviews. Making their home in Texas, she and her husband, Pastor Tom Faile, enjoy spending time with family, friends, and traveling.

Scott Goodfellow is the Lead Pastor at Granbury First United Methodist Church. He is a fully trained leadership and executive coach. You can follow Scott on Instagram @scottjgoodfellow. He lives in Texas with his wife, Christy.